He was only seven weeks old when he made them.

Actually, Mosi didn't want to open his hands,

so they are more like fist prints!

Mosi Musa

A True Tale about a Baby Monkey Raised by His Grandma
by Georgeanne Irvine

Published by SAN DIEGO ZOO GLOBAL PRESS

Mosi Musa: A True Tale about a Baby Monkey Raised by His Grandma was published by San Diego Zoo Global Press in association with Blue Sneaker Press. Through these publishing efforts, we seek to inspire multiple generations to care about wildlife, the natural world, and conservation.

San Diego Zoo Global is committed to leading the fight against extinction. It saves species worldwide by uniting its expertise in animal care and conservation science with its dedication to inspire a passion for nature.

Douglas G. Myers, President and Chief Executive Officer
Shawn Dixon, Chief Operating Officer
Yvonne Miles, Corporate Director of Retail
Georgeanne Irvine, Director of Corporate Publishing
San Diego Zoo Global
P.O. Box 120551
San Diego, CA 92112-0551
sandiegozoo.org | 619-231-1515

San Diego Zoo Global's publishing partner is Blue Sneaker Press, an imprint of Southwestern Publishing Group, Inc., 2451 Atrium Way, Nashville, TN 37214. Southwestern Publishing Group is a wholly owned subsidiary of Southwestern Family of Companies, Nashville, Tennessee.

Christopher G. Capen, President, Southwestern Publishing Group
Carrie Hasler, Publisher, Blue Sneaker Press
Kristin Connelly, Managing Editor
Lori Sandstrom, Art Director/Graphic Designer
swpublishinggroup.com | 800-358-0560

ISBN: 978-1-943198-09-2
Library of Congress Control Number: 2019937463
Printed in China
10 9 8 7 6 5 4 3 2 1

To precious
Mosi Musa **and** his grandma Thelma
**and to grandmothers everywhere
who love their grandchildren.**

Acknowledgments:

IT TAKES A VILLAGE TO CREATE A BOOK LIKE THIS—MY DEEPEST APPRECIATION TO
THE FOLLOWING PEOPLE, WHO ARE ALL A PART OF THAT VILLAGE:

Janet Hawes, April Rearick, Jasmine Almonte-Crouse, Dean Gibson, Marianne Zeitz, Brian Opitz,
Pat Morris, DVM, Kim Weibel, Becky Kier, Joanne Mills, Jill Andrews, Kim Livingstone, Sue Averill,
Serena Gill, Mary Dural, Rochelle Willison, Julian Castellanos, Cathy Wertis, Lori Sandstrom,
Carrie Hasler, Yvonne Miles, Mary Sekulovich, Ken Bohn, Tammy Spratt, Lisa Bissi, Jen MacEwen,
Kim Turner, Douglas Myers, Shawn Dixon, Chris Capen, Angel Chambosse, and Cheryl Hornbaker.

PHOTO CREDITS
Ken Bohn: 8 right, 11, 12, 13, 14, 15, 16, 17 upper left and lower left, 18 bottom right, 19, 28 lower, 29.
Tammy Spratt: front and back covers, front jacket flap, title page, 3, 4, 10 right, 24 left, 27 middle,
28 upper, 31, 32, 33. **Georgeanne Irvine:** 18 left, 20, 21, 22, 23, 25, 26, 27 upper and lower, 30.
Dean Gibson: 8 left, 9, 10 upper. **April Rearick:** 5, 24 right. **Jill Andrews:** 6, 10 middle. **Marianne Zeitz:** 7.
Janet Hawes: 17 upper right. **Angel Chambosse:** back jacket flap. **Shutterstock:** 34, 35, 36.

A Baby Monkey Is on the Way!

Primate keepers at the San Diego Zoo watched as Louise, a vervet monkey, tenderly cradled a big brown ball in her arms. Louise was expecting a baby any day. Her keepers hoped Louise would be a good mother because she carried the ball with her everywhere and cuddled it like an infant.

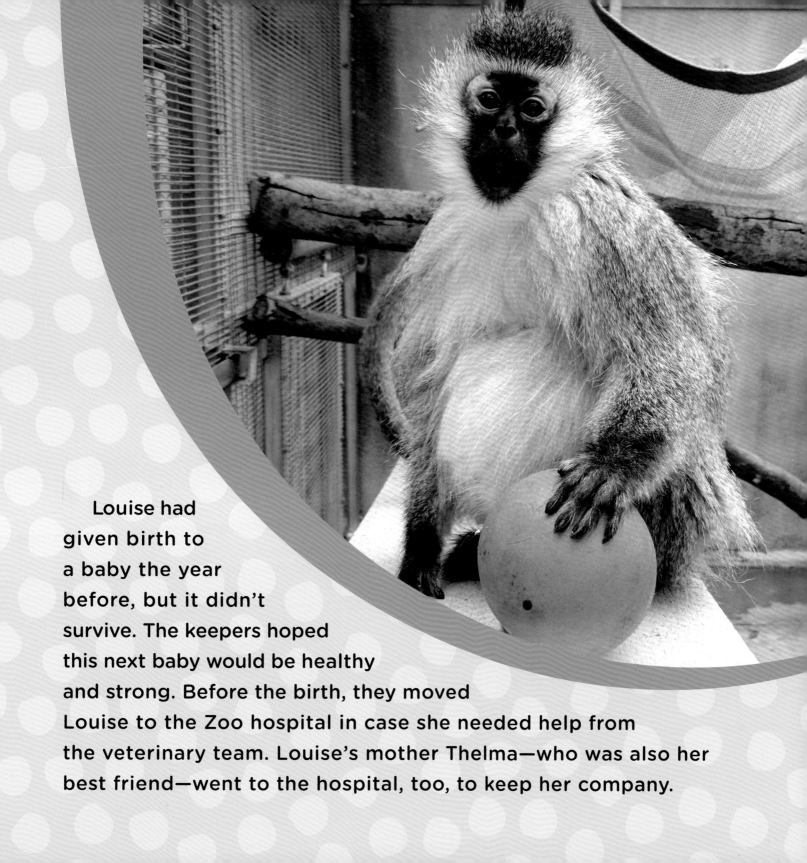

Louise had given birth to a baby the year before, but it didn't survive. The keepers hoped this next baby would be healthy and strong. Before the birth, they moved Louise to the Zoo hospital in case she needed help from the veterinary team. Louise's mother Thelma—who was also her best friend—went to the hospital, too, to keep her company.

When it was time for Louise to have her baby, something was terribly wrong with her. The veterinarian knew that if he didn't help Louise, she *and* her baby might die! Louise was given medicine to make her go to sleep. Then the veterinarian made a small cut in Louise's belly and took the baby out. "It's a boy!" he said.

Soon after the baby vervet monkey was born, he made cooing sounds.

The tiny monkey's heart was beating, but he wasn't breathing yet. A veterinary nurse massaged the baby's chest, and after 20 seconds, he took his first breath! Everyone cheered! Within seven minutes, the baby opened his eyes, and then the team did a high five.

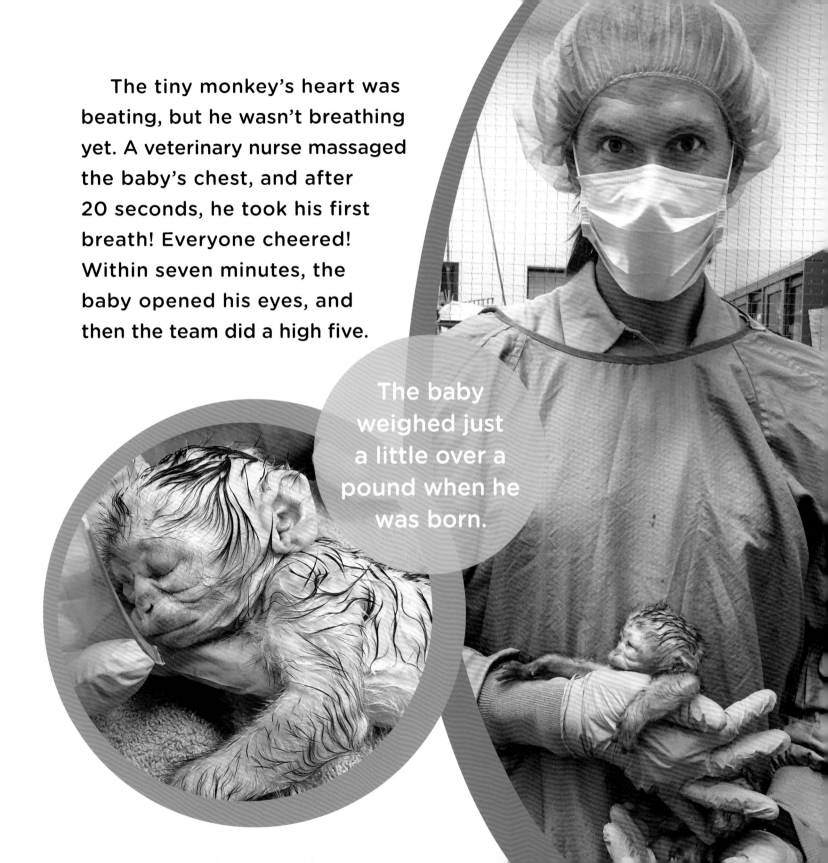

The baby weighed just a little over a pound when he was born.

Introducing Mosi

The baby was named Mosi Musa (Mōsee Moo-suh). He was placed next to Louise, so she could see him as soon as she woke up. Keepers hoped that Louise would accept her new son, but that didn't happen. When she opened her eyes, Louise pushed Mosi Musa away. It became clear that she wasn't interested in caring for her newborn baby.

THELMA

Mosi Musa means "first born" in Swahili. His nickname is Mosi.

Grandma Thelma was eager to meet Mosi, though. The first time Thelma saw him, she smacked her lips and reached out to touch him. That meant she liked him and wanted to hold him close to her.

To keep little Mosi warm, he was placed in an incubator where Louise and Thelma could see him. Whenever nursery keepers fed Mosi milk formula from a bottle, they let Mosi's mother and his grandmother watch them. After Mosi finished eating, his keeper gently rubbed his back so he would burp.

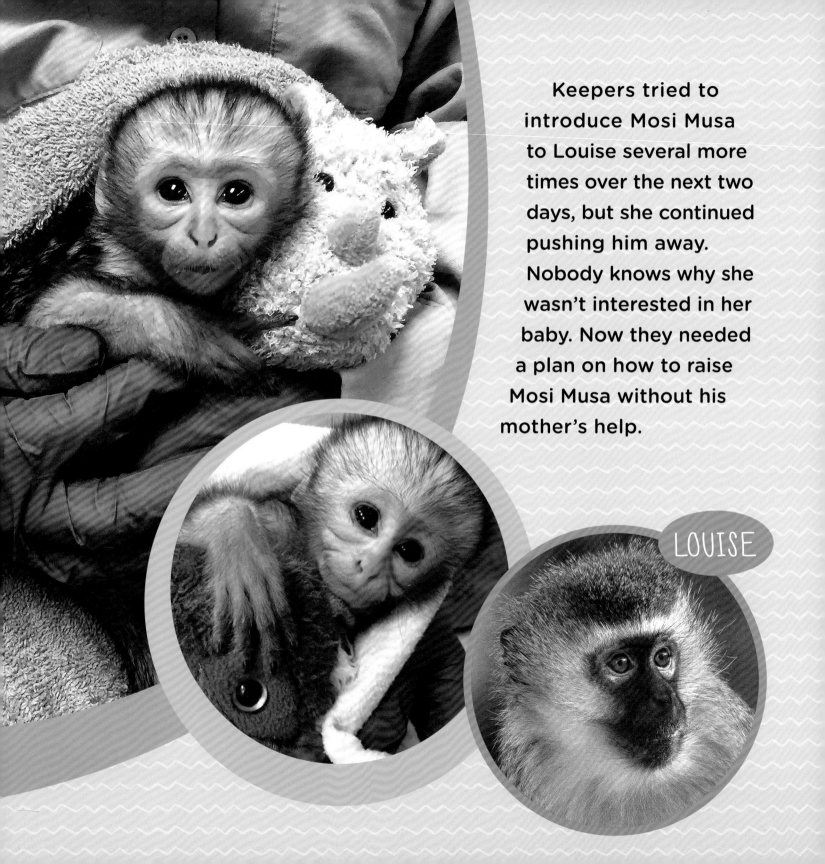

Keepers tried to introduce Mosi Musa to Louise several more times over the next two days, but she continued pushing him away. Nobody knows why she wasn't interested in her baby. Now they needed a plan on how to raise Mosi Musa without his mother's help.

LOUISE

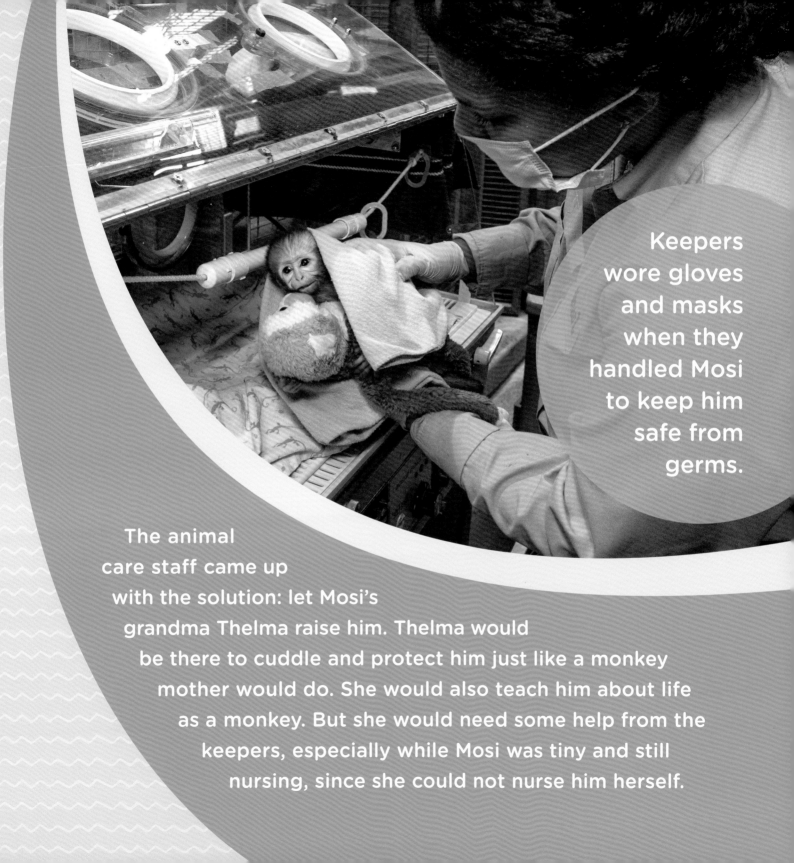

Keepers wore gloves and masks when they handled Mosi to keep him safe from germs.

The animal care staff came up with the solution: let Mosi's grandma Thelma raise him. Thelma would be there to cuddle and protect him just like a monkey mother would do. She would also teach him about life as a monkey. But she would need some help from the keepers, especially while Mosi was tiny and still nursing, since she could not nurse him herself.

Cuddling with Grandma

Mosi was five days old when his keepers moved him, along with Thelma and Louise, from the hospital to a behind-the-scenes area in the Zoo. There, Grandma Thelma cuddled Mosi for the first time—and he clung to her tightly.

As Mosi got older and stronger, he would get to spend longer periods of time with Thelma.

Even though Thelma and Mosi liked being together, he couldn't stay with her all the time yet. Keepers needed to feed him milk formula eight times a day. When Mosi wasn't with his grandma, he snuggled with his favorite toys: a fuzzy rhinoceros and a monkey.

When keepers wanted to give Mosi to Thelma for snuggling and grandma time, they put him in what they called the "howdy chute." It was a small pen with two doors: one opened into Thelma's area and the other opened into the hallway where Mosi's incubator was located. After Mosi was fed, his keeper placed him in the chute, then closed the hallway door and opened Thelma's door. She always waited for Mosi at the door, quickly scooping him up in her arms.

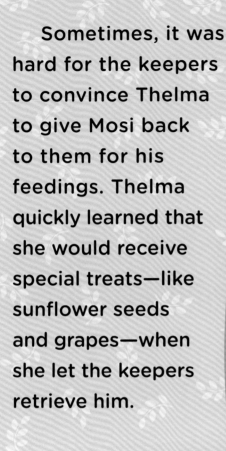

Sometimes, it was hard for the keepers to convince Thelma to give Mosi back to them for his feedings. Thelma quickly learned that she would receive special treats—like sunflower seeds and grapes—when she let the keepers retrieve him.

Vinny, Mosi's father, lived in the behind-the-scenes monkey area, too. He and Mosi could see each other through a mesh door that separated them. Mosi would get to meet his dad when he was a little older.

Mosi's incubator was filled with toys. He was playful, curious, and sometimes silly. If he wasn't snuggling with his stuffed animals, he was leaping around and exercising on his pull-up bar. The tiny monkey became stronger and more confident every day!

Growing Stronger Every Day

Mosi's teeth started growing in when he was two weeks old—then he chewed on everything!

Mosi got plenty of fresh air and sunshine, too. On warm days, he played in an outdoor pen, which had small tree branches in it so he could learn to climb. As an adult, he would spend lots of time in the treetops.

Mosi made
lots of
funny faces.

Climbing up was easy,
but getting down was harder.
The first time Mosi crawled to the top
of a branch, he chirped and purred because
he was scared. He wasn't sure how to get
down. Thelma, who was nearby, chattered.
She was concerned about Mosi. Keeper
Jasmine rushed to help and comfort him.
He wasn't afraid to climb again, though,
and got braver the more he practiced.

By the time Mosi was three weeks old, he moved to a much larger space with even more toys and taller branches. He easily scrambled from the lowest branch to the highest branch and back down again.

Keeper Jasmine took him on a field trip to a huge outdoor enclosure where the grown-up monkeys played together.

Grandma Thelma watched Mosi and Jasmine through a window.

The keepers liked seeing Mosi grow up and become more sure of himself.

Mosi clung to his favorite toy monkey at first. It gave him comfort when his grandma wasn't there. Once Mosi became more at ease in the new area, he hopped from branch to branch, pausing every once in a while to chew on a leaf.

Mealtime for Mosi

Mosi's favorite part of the day was feeding time. He loved his milk bottle and jumped up and down when it was time to eat. Mosi was sweet and friendly most of the time, but every so often, he threw a tantrum!

Mosi liked to eat so much that his keepers called him a chowhound.

Once when he was extra hungry, he got angry when his keeper didn't pick him up fast enough to feed him. Another time, he was unhappy when he finished his bottle because he wanted more!

The keepers enjoyed working with Mosi, even when he was a little fussy. The spunky baby monkey held a very special place in everyone's hearts.

Some
monkeys,
like vervets,
have a pouch
in their cheeks
to stash and
store food.

As Mosi grew older, he was introduced to solid foods like dried cranberries, grapes, broccoli, and sunflower seeds. Keeper Kim would offer him bits of food which he would gobble up. One day, she gave him a square piece of jicama. Mosi stuffed it in his cheek pouch to save as a snack for later, when he was back with Grandma Thelma. Kim smiled because she could see the square outline of the jicama in Mosi's bulging cheek.

Mosi sometimes sucked his thumb, just like a human infant does.

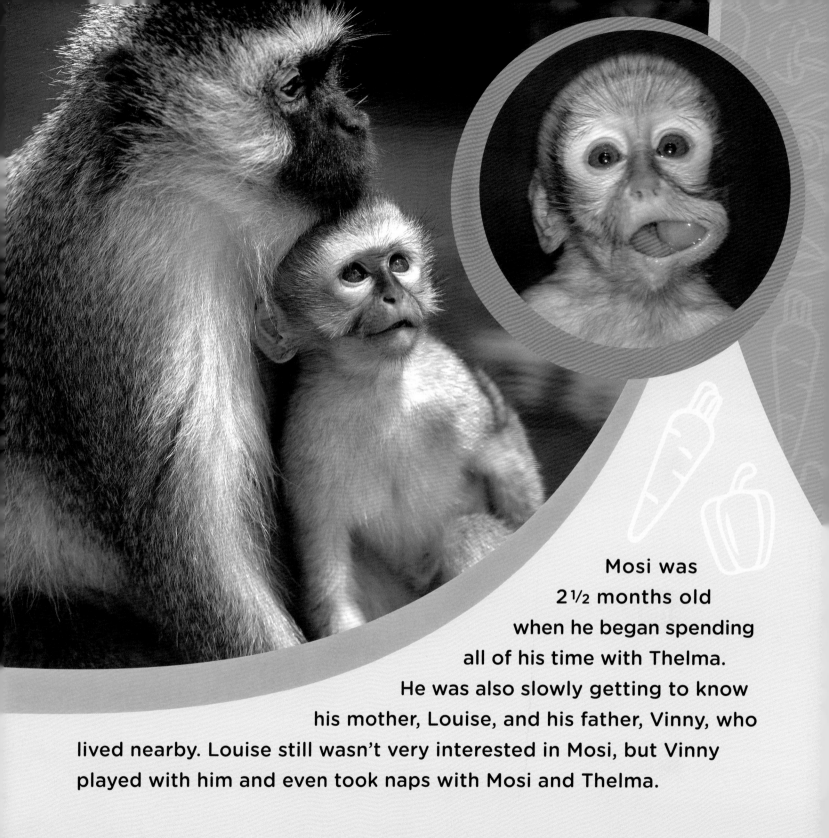

Mosi was
2½ months old
when he began spending
all of his time with Thelma.
He was also slowly getting to know
his mother, Louise, and his father, Vinny, who
lived nearby. Louise still wasn't very interested in Mosi, but Vinny
played with him and even took naps with Mosi and Thelma.

Mosi ate mostly solid food now—just like his grandma—but still drank a few bottles of milk each day. When it was time to eat, keepers called his name. He sometimes had to wrestle himself away from Thelma. She was protective and didn't always want to let him go. Mosi would scamper to the edge of his enclosure. He stayed inside while his keepers fed him from the hallway. Mosi often tried to hold the bottle himself or wrapped his tiny hand around his keeper's finger while he ate.

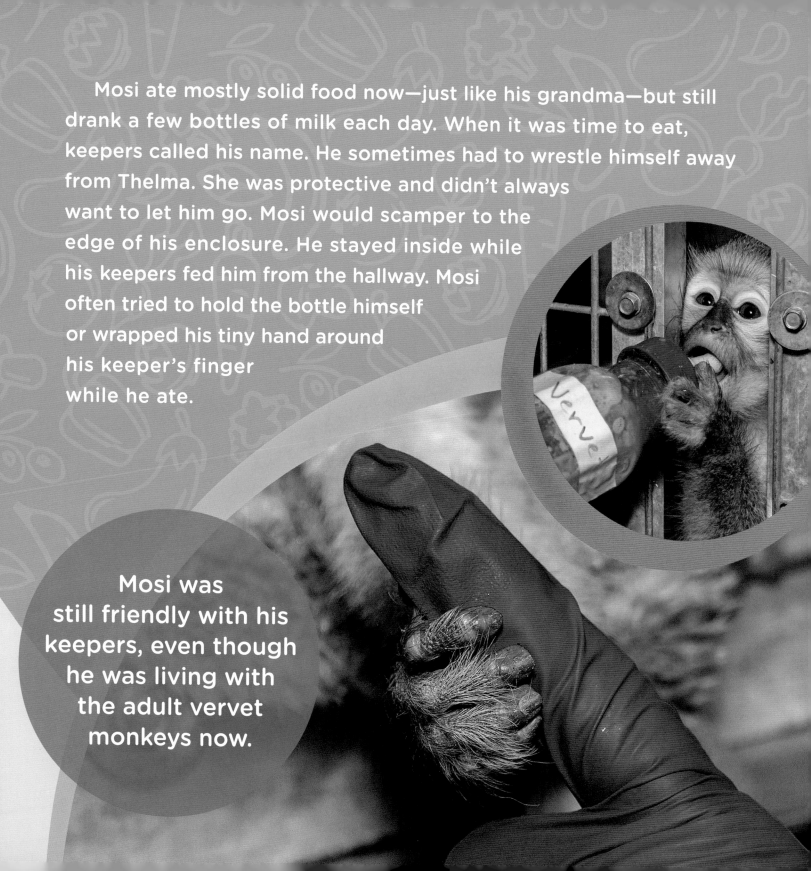

Mosi was still friendly with his keepers, even though he was living with the adult vervet monkeys now.

Monkey Moving Day

Life was about to change for Mosi, Thelma, and their family: it was time to move to their spacious new home in the Zoo's Africa Rocks habitat.

Keepers coaxed Mosi and Thelma into a travel kennel with treats. Mosi stayed close to his grandma because he was unsure of what was happening. Then he became curious and watched as Louise and Vinny were carried out in their kennels.

The van that transported Mosi and his family to Africa Rocks was nicknamed the "monkey mobile."

SAN DIEGO ZOO
PRIMATE DEPARTMENT

When they were loaded in a van for the short trip, Mosi clung to Thelma once again. With his grandma by his side, he felt secure in this unusual situation.

Mosi and his family spent the first day at their new home in an indoor area to get used to their surroundings. Mosi was still a little scared, but Thelma was close by in case he needed a hug.

CONRAD PREBYS
AFRICA ROCKS

Home in the Trees

The next morning, a door slid open so Mosi, Thelma, Louise, and Vinny could go outside into their new forested home. Keeper April had placed food deep into the exhibit, hoping to draw the monkeys out to explore.

Mosi rode on Thelma's back, peeking around the corner of the rocks as they entered the exhibit. They retreated back to the bedroom a few times, but they stayed out longer each time as they became more comfortable.

Finally, Mosi's curiosity got the best of him. He jumped off Thelma's back, bravely running and leaping through the exhibit, exploring every inch of it. He scrambled up a tree, climbed through the leaves, and even swung on a branch like a grown-up monkey.

Mosi's new next-door neighbors were leopards on one side and lemurs on the other.

Mosi Fits In

One day, shortly after they moved in, Mosi and his grandma Thelma sat together on a big rock. Louise had been carrying her brown ball around for most of the morning. Suddenly, Louise set the ball down to climb up next to Mosi. Then she started grooming him, which is what monkeys do when they want to be friends. Mosi's mother was finally paying attention to him and accepting him into the family!

Grooming each other helps strengthen bonds between vervet monkeys.

When the
grooming session was
finished, Mosi scampered up a
tree to chew on a few leaves. He leapt out of
the tree to snuggle with Grandma Thelma for a few minutes. Next,
he climbed back up the tree to look at the Zoo visitors, who were
admiring his acrobatics.

As Mosi's keepers watched him exploring and enjoying his new home, they smiled. Mosi had needed a helping hand from human caretakers until he was nearly six months old, but now he lives full time with his vervet monkey family. He doesn't need his bottle anymore, either.

The keepers felt happy—they knew that Mosi has all the confidence he needs to live an enriching life. One other thing they knew: Mosi will always have a special bond with Thelma, his grandma who cared for him right from the start!

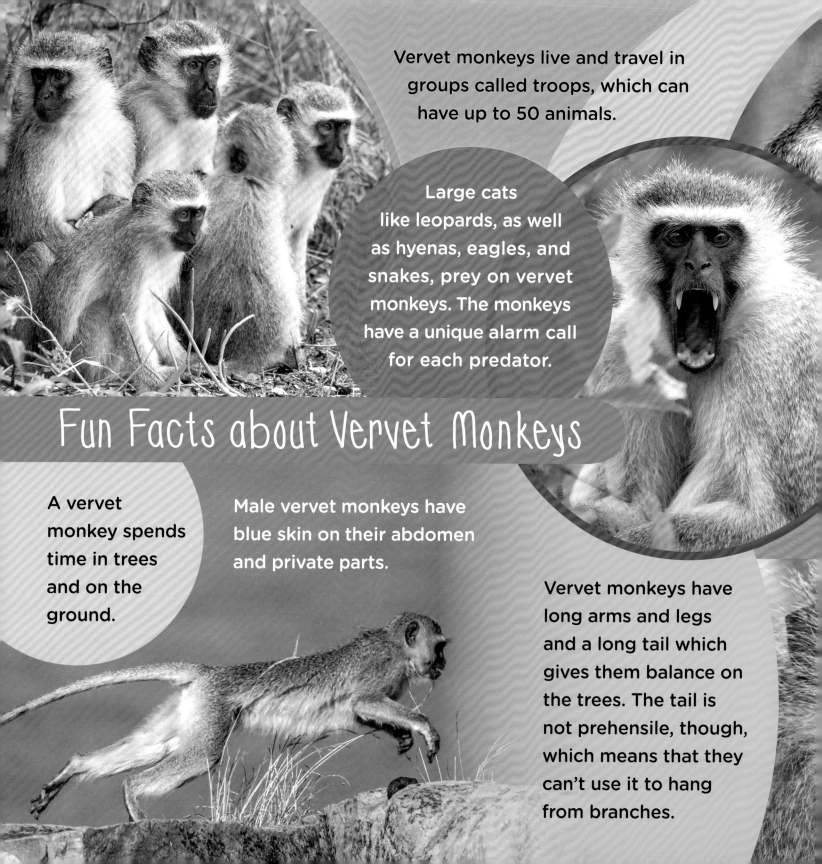

Vervet monkeys live and travel in groups called troops, which can have up to 50 animals.

Large cats like leopards, as well as hyenas, eagles, and snakes, prey on vervet monkeys. The monkeys have a unique alarm call for each predator.

Fun Facts about Vervet Monkeys

A vervet monkey spends time in trees and on the ground.

Male vervet monkeys have blue skin on their abdomen and private parts.

Vervet monkeys have long arms and legs and a long tail which gives them balance on the trees. The tail is not prehensile, though, which means that they can't use it to hang from branches.

Typically, only one baby vervet monkey is born at a time; twins are uncommon.

Vervet monkeys can live up to 30 years in some zoos.

Vervet monkeys groom one another by picking through each other's hair, looking for dirt, flakes of dry skin, and small insects like lice and ticks.

Vervet monkeys are omnivores—they eat a variety of foods such as leaves, seeds, fruits, flowers, bird eggs, and lizards.

Vervet monkeys are diurnal, which means they are active during the day and sleep at night.

Where Vervet Monkeys Like Mosi Live

AFRICA

Atlantic Ocean

Indian Ocean

CURRENTLY, VERVET MONKEYS ARE NOT ENDANGERED IN THE WILD, BUT HUMANS ARE A BIG THREAT TO THEM.

Threats to Vervet Monkeys:

- Habitat loss, including forests that are being replaced with farmland

- Being killed by farmers, who see vervets as pests because the monkeys raid their crops to survive

- Hunting for their meat

- Trapping to be sold as pets or used in scientific experiments

How You Can Help:

To learn how you can be a superhero for vervet monkeys and other wildlife as well as help lead the fight against extinction, visit:

sandiegozookids.org/save-animals

and

endextinction.org

Special Note:
After this book was written, Grandma Thelma died peacefully with Mosi, Louise, and Vinny by her side.

These are Mosi's footprints!

Vervet monkeys are excellent climbers.